THE ADULT'S ZODIAC COLORING STORYBOOK

Explore the Mythic World of the Zodiac,
One Colorful Page at a Time

D. M. STRANGE

1231 Publishing
PO Box 77
Kallangur QLD 4503
AUSTRALIA

Fiction © 2024 D M Strange
Illustrations may be copied and shared

All rights reserved. The stories found in this book, or any portion thereof may not be reproduced in any manner whatsoever without the express written permission of the publisher, 1231 Publishing, except for the use of brief quotations in a book review.

ISBN: 978-1-7637236-6-5

This book can be ordered directly from the publisher 1231publishing.com
or from your local or online bookshop.

Hello Artist of Colors,

I've always been fascinated by star signs.

I'm very typical of my Taurean sign, and my closest friends and family are very typical of their signs. I do believe that everything is connected, from the place we were born down to the second.

I want to share something I find super cool: Quantum mechanics suggests that everything in the universe, including particles and waves, is interconnected through a web of energy. Nobody has all the answers, but many of us can see the patterns. From scientists to astrologers.

The stories here are each inspired by one of the pictures. I wrote the story for the picture, rather than the other way around. I own a few art books, and when I look through them, I'll think up a little story or fantasy to go along with the artwork. I did the same here.

You'll find twelve stories, one for each of the signs. In each story, I've fit in as many traits and symbols for that star sign as I could, which was both a challenge and some extra fun for me. Perhaps you'll have fun finding all the symbolism and traits. Perhaps you'll read the story for what it is—just a story. Either way, I hope they bring you joy.

The pictures were designed using specifications that I plugged into AI software. I discarded anything that didn't fit or look good for coloring. I used keywords and descriptions specific to the sign, but I didn't always use symbolism. For example, for Cancer I did use the crab, but there are also images honoring home, family and the moon, which are important representations of a Cancerian.

I recommend using pencils, crayons, pastels or ballpoints because the images are on both sides of the paper. Paints and/or markers will seep through.

Whether you're coloring for fun, curiosity, relaxation, de-stressing, mindfulness, or focus exercises, I hope these illustrations and stories entertain you.

All the best,

D.

Fire and Horn

The dawn sky burned red as Althea strode across the rugged borderlands, spear in hand, gaze fierce and unyielding. By her side, Mars, her faithful ram, bounded over the rocky terrain, his horns gleaming like polished bronze. Together, they were a force of fire and determination—a living embodiment of the Aries spirit. Althea's heart beat with the pulse of the first sign, driven by courage, raw as the rising sun, and an unending need to forge her own path.

Her people spoke of her as the ram-headed guardian. Every day, she patrolled the borders with Mars, her eyes seeking signs of danger, her instincts sharp. She fought with ferocity, her spirit untamed and her heart aflame with devotion to her kin. When threats loomed, she met them head-on, her movements swift, her spear striking true—each thrust propelled by the unstoppable force of Aries.

The ram was her companion in every battle, embodying her determination. He charged forward with her, hooves pounding the earth like a war drum, a battering ram of nature's might. Together, they knew no fear. Althea's laughter echoed across the hills as they trained, Mars ramming into practice dummies as she sparred with the shadows cast by the morning sun.

The two moved as one, fire and horn, energy and strength, with a bond forged under the stars—undaunted by any foe, unyielding to any challenge. Together, they were the ram's spirit incarnate, fierce guardians of the land they loved.

The Woman Who Moved Mountains

In the heart of a small village lived Zurah, whose power to shape the earth made her both revered and feared. Her hands, rough as the soil she commanded, bore the resilience of Taurus, her spirit bound to the earth beneath her feet. People came from across the kingdom, seeking her touch—to move rivers that had run dry, to carve valleys that might cradle lakes and bring life to barren lands. She listened with a Taurean patience, always willing to shape and shelter, to nurture and protect.

Zurah's magic was not borne of dark rituals but of an ancient connection to the land. Her power was the blessing of Venus, the same force that brought the pink roses to bloom at her cottage door, that made her garden overflow with abundance. She was the Bull's daughter—loyal, steady, and fiercely protective of her home.

One day, men arrived from a distant town, their faces twisted in fear and hatred. They called her witch, spat venomous words, and raised their torches against her. Zurah watched them, her eyes heavy with the quiet force of her sign. With a whispered command, the earth beneath the men opened, a gaping mouth swallowing them whole. They sank, their cries muffled by layers of soil until silence returned.

Zurah looked at the ground, now smooth and unbroken, her heart untroubled. The Bull protects its own, she thought, turning back to her garden. The earth, steadfast as ever, would always listen to her, and she to it—a bond unbroken.

Breathless

The morning was bright, sunlight spilling through the trees like golden laughter. It was exactly the kind of day that made Eliza itch to move. She turned to her twin sister, Clara, whose reluctance was evident in the slow, thoughtful way she laced her hiking boots. The Gemini twins—one energetic and boundless, the other cautious and contemplative.

"I don't know, Eliza," Clara murmured. "What if my blood sugar drops too low? Or I get too tired?"

Eliza, ever the twin with the quicksilver smile and Gemini's boundless energy, knelt beside her sister. She rested a reassuring hand on Clara's knee. "I'll carry everything you need, promise. Snacks, water, your glucometer—all of it. I just don't want you to miss this." Her eyes were bright, twinkling with determination.

Clara sighed but nodded. Together, they set off—Eliza leading with her light steps and chatter, Clara following, steady and careful.

The climb was not easy. Clara paused to catch her breath, her body reminding her of its limits. But Eliza was there, offering snacks, water and a gentle hand when the trail steepened. They were two halves of the celestial whole, each compensating for the other's weaknesses.

When they reached the summit, Clara was breathless, but not from exhaustion. The vista below—green valleys, silver rivers—was worth every step. Eliza turned to her, wrapping an arm around her shoulders.

"See? I knew you could do it," she said, her voice full of Gemini warmth. Clara smiled, her heart full. Together, they stood at the peak, twin spirits united, gazing at the world they could conquer—side by side.

Moonlit Tides and Coral Dreams

Crab lived a quiet life, tucked in his sandy burrow beneath the dune grass. It was simple, perhaps even dull, but it was his—the safe and familiar home of a Cancer soul. He scuttled out each morning, feeling the tide's pull, the soft glow of the moon whispering comfort to him. Though his claws longed for adventure, Crab had grown content with his snug home.

One day, while wandering the beach, a shadow fell over him. He was plucked from the sand by a sharp-beaked seagull, his claws helplessly dangling as he was lifted into the sky. The wind howled in his ears, and Crab's heart pounded with fear. This, he thought, was surely the end.

But another gull, seeing its rival's prize, swooped in, shrieking for a share. In the struggle, Crab was dropped, tumbling end over end until he splashed into the ocean below. For a moment, he was lost—disoriented, spinning in a cloud of bubbles. The familiar tides now roared around him, pulling him down, down.

When he could finally make sense of what he was seeing, the world had changed. Bright coral forests surrounded him, fish glimmered in colors he'd never imagined, and sea anemones swayed like lanterns. It was a place of life and beauty—a home filled with the nurturing energy of Cancer, tinged with wonder.

Crab settled among the coral, his heart swollen with joy. Here, in the magic of the underwater world, he found not just safety, but the adventure he'd never dared to seek. It was a new home, brimming with life, vibrant as the moonlit tides that had always guided him.

The Golden Cage

The King of the Sun lived in a palace of light, adored by all. Every day, his subjects praised his beauty, strength, and power. They cheered for his radiant presence, never questioning his reign, never doubting the wisdom of his rule. His light was their guidance, and his golden palace their hope.

But for the King, the glow had begun to dim. His days were a repetition of praises and ceremonial duties, and his nights were spent in restless contemplation. He was the beacon of the realm, yet he longed for something more—something different, away from the constant glare.

One night, his sister and adviser, Seraphine, approached him. She was a proud woman, sharp-witted and calculating, who'd spent years in his shadow. "Brother," she said, her voice a whisper of promise, "I have discovered a portal—a gateway to the world beyond our palace. Beyond it lies true freedom, far from this golden cage."

The King's heart surged at her words. Freedom. It was all he'd wished for. Without hesitation, he followed Seraphine through the darkened halls to a hidden archway, shimmering faintly. The portal.

"As King, you must go first," Seraphine said, her eyes unreadable. "Claim the world beyond."

The King stepped through the portal, a smile of hope on his lips—only to find himself suspended in an endless dark void. No light, no warmth, only silence. He turned, but the portal behind him had vanished, sealing him within nothingness.

On the other side, Seraphine watched the gateway close. She turned, her eyes catching the golden glimmer of the throne. Slowly, she ascended the steps and sat, her fingers curling around the armrests.

The throne was hers now. And Seraphine smiled—ready to radiate her own light across the lands.

The Case of the Muddy Boots

Detective Mei Lin stood in front of the lineup; four men arranged like a garden of secrets waiting to be unearthed. They were groundskeepers, every one of them employed by the council to tend to the public gardens. Somewhere among the mud-smeared boots and nervous glances was the murderer. The police stood behind her, rigid and ready, the tension palpable in the chilly morning air.

Mei turned to the constable beside her. "Bring me a couple of buckets of water," she instructed. Mei was known for her meticulous attention to detail, a hallmark of her Virgo nature. The men shifted uncomfortably, their eyes widening as her request was carried out. She was known for her unorthodox methods, and today would be no different.

The constable returned, two buckets sloshing with cold water. "Take off your boots, gentlemen," she ordered. Each man hesitated before bending to unlace their mud-caked boots, placing them carefully before them. They were uniform—standard-issue, sturdy boots, designed for work. The police had chatted amongst themselves, saying there were no clues there, but she knew different.

Mei knelt, her methodical nature guiding her actions. She dipped a rag into the water, scrubbing at the first pair of boots, revealing only a layer of well-worn tread. She moved to the second—again, nothing unusual. Then, the third pair. As she cleaned away the dirt, a pebble revealed itself, wedged into the sole, leaving a distinctive mark. Her heart quickened, but her expression remained composed. She compared the imprint to the drawing she'd made of the footprint left behind at the scene—it was a perfect match.

She stood, meeting the third gardener's eyes with a steady gaze. "Arrest him," she said softly, gesturing to the constables. Mei's precision and analytical mind had led her to the truth. The man's face crumpled, and he began to weep. "It was an accident," he plead as they led him away.

Mei watched, her gaze steady, her mind already analyzing the next steps. Accidents or not, the truth

always found a way through the mud. Her diligence and devotion to justice—true Virgo qualities—had once again ensured that order was restored.

Sands of Time

The adventurer's party trudged deeper into the cavern, their footsteps echoing off jagged walls. Leading them was Thorne, whose calm demeanor and sense of fairness kept the group moving despite growing doubts. He insisted they take the right path at the first fork, even when the road seemed perilous. The left path, more peaceful and inviting, tempted the group, but Thorne's insistence never wavered.

"Trust me," he urged. The others exchanged glances, their trust wavering. Thorne always sought harmony within the group, but his evasiveness was now sowing seeds of discord.

Nala, their tracker, frowned. "Thorne, how do you know this is the right way?" she asked.

"I just know," Thorne replied, avoiding conflict. They climbed upward, choosing risk over ease. Eventually, they squeezed through a narrow tunnel, emerging into a wide grotto. A shimmering ceiling sparkled above a black lake, the scene breathtakingly beautiful—a reminder of Libra's affinity for beauty and balance.

In the lake's center, upon a platform, stood an hourglass, glowing faintly. Brian started toward the water, but Thorne stopped him, his voice authoritative. "Don't touch the water. There are creatures beneath—one bite, and they could have half of you."

Brian stared at him. "How do you know?"

Thorne's gaze became vulnerable. "It happened to me. I lost both my legs swimming to the hourglass, but I made it. Somehow, I made it. I used it to turn back time and save myself. Not just me," he added, his voice trembling, "all of you. You all died, either falling or were trapped. I kept going and used the hourglass to restore balance. I think I'm the only one who remembers because I was the one who turned the hourglass."

They stared at the hourglass, horror dawning.

No Cameras, No Mercy

Lisa and Madison sat on the porch of Madison's home, the night sky above them dark and deep as a Scorpio's secretive soul. The air was heavy with the mystery of untold truths, and the wind carried a cool intensity.

"It was such a great job," Lisa sighed, shaking her head. "But working with him made it unbearable. All the harassment, the constant manipulation. I should've known better. The red flag was right there—every woman eventually quit." Her voice turned venomous, echoing a grudge held close to the heart.

Madison listened quietly, her lips curved into a small, knowing smile. Her eyes had a gleam that reflected something deeper than what was spoken—an intensity hidden beneath her calm facade.

Lisa looked over at her friend. "Honestly, I still can't believe how you managed to put up with it after I left," she said, genuine concern touching her voice.

Madison's smile widened. "It wasn't long after you left that he died, you know. Hit by a truck."

Lisa blinked, her mind wandering back to the news story. She remembered reading the headline, a mix of shock and strange satisfaction coursing through her. "Yeah, I remember. It was all over the news. Still can't believe nobody had any footage of it—everyone's always got their phones out."

Madison let out a soft laugh, the kind of laugh that curled like smoke—mysterious and dangerous. "Just as well," she said.

Lisa frowned slightly, tilting her head. "Why's that?"

Madison's eyes glinted, a predatory smile crossing her face. "Because I'm the one who pushed him."

Embers of Friendship

The campfire flickered, sending sparks spiraling into the star-filled sky. The group of friends sat around it, laughter bubbling up between them, their breath fogging in the crisp night air. They were Sagittarians at heart—adventurers on the verge of new frontiers. University graduation loomed, their separate paths about to unfurl across different cities, careers, and even continents. But tonight, they were here, together, under the wide sky that spoke of limitless horizons.

Maya raised a bottle, grinning. "To adventure!" she called, and they clinked their drinks, echoes of their cheer spreading into the forest. A moment of silence fell as they each looked into the fire, flames mirrored in their eyes. They were hopeful, optimistic, yearning for the next great journey, yet acutely aware of what they were about to leave behind.

"Think we'll keep in touch?" asked Sam, a wistful smile touching his lips. He was destined for a career in a distant city, and though his heart burned with excitement, a tinge of sadness colored his words.

"Of course we will," Maya said, her voice full of conviction. "We'll all find each other again… somewhere out there." She gestured broadly at the horizon, the expansive sky beyond them, as if their bonds were as boundless as the universe itself.

For now, there was only this: the freedom of the wilderness, the camaraderie of friends, and the embers of a fire slowly fading. They laughed again, speaking of places they would see, the risks they would take. There was wanderlust in their veins, and though uncertainty lay ahead, they embraced it, knowing life was one grand adventure.

Love's Gambit

Every weekend, the chessboard sat between them in the park, squares of black and white illuminated by the morning sun. The mother, Denise, watched her daughter, Amara, contemplate her next move. Denise had always been pragmatic, grounded, her Capricorn spirit built on steady ambitions, relentless hard work, and resilience. But Amara—Amara was the best of all her hopes made real.

Denise wanted more for her daughter than she'd dared to dream for herself. Her own childhood had been a landscape of obstacles: financial hardships, sacrifices, doors closed before they were even approached. She'd clawed her way to a stable life through determination, never losing sight of her goal to provide a foundation and opportunities for her child.

As Amara's hand hovered over her rook, Denise smiled, her heart swelling with love and quiet pride. Chess was more than a game to them. It was a symbol—of strategy, patience, and persistence, qualities Denise knew would serve her daughter in life. She wanted Amara to learn how to think ahead, how to see the broader picture, how to stay resilient even when the world seemed ready to topple the queen that she was.

Amara moved her rook, then looked up, her eyes bright. "Your turn," she said, her voice filled with a joy that warmed Denise from the inside out.

Denise leaned forward, her fingers brushing a knight, considering her options. "Remember, baby," she said softly, "you can build something strong if you're patient." She looked at her daughter, hoping she could somehow convey all the lessons she wished she'd been taught. Ambition tempered by compassion, success built on a foundation of love.

The game continued as the sun rose higher, and Denise felt it—a future as promising as the bright sky above them, limitless for her daughter.

The Secret Miracle

Every month, the woman journeyed deep into the forest, taking secret winding paths that twisted unpredictably, to reach the magic lagoon. The water shimmered like liquid starlight, glowing electric blue, speaking of distant galaxies and infinite possibilities. She filled her jug carefully and brought it back to her village. The water healed wounds and revived the sick, flowing like a current of hope. The villagers depended on her miracles.

One evening, as she returned, not far from the village and with the jug cradled in her arms, she was confronted by three men blocking her path. Their eyes were filled with desperate intensity. "Please," one of them said, voice breaking, "show us where the lagoon is. Our families are sick. We need more than what you bring."

She shook her head. "I cannot. If too many find it, the lagoon will lose its power."

Their desperation sparked into anger. The tallest man stepped forward, voice trembling. "Please, you don't understand. My son is dying."

Her heart broke for their pain but she stood firm. "The balance must be kept. The lagoon's power comes from its rarity—too many hands would only snuff it out."

The tall man's face twisted. "Then what good are you?" In a swift, terrible motion, he drew a knife and stabbed her. She crumpled, the jug slipping from her grasp.

The other two men gasped, horrified. They grabbed the jug before it spilled all its contents and poured what was left of the magic water over her wound. It did nothing. She smiled faintly, whispering, "The lagoon... I am it and it is me. It will be a secret forever now."

Her body shimmered, transforming into silvery liquid and soaking into the earth, leaving nothing behind but silence and regret.

Echoes of the Past

The grand foyer was her favorite place to play; the marble floor cool beneath her feet, its expansiveness reflecting the emptiness she'd always felt about her past. She played her harp alone, delicate notes spilling like ripples on a lake—not only vibrating outwards, but clear, soft, and filled with yearning. As her fingers brushed each string, the sound echoed against the tall windows and spiraled towards the arched ceiling, filling every forgotten corner of the room with her ethereal song.

The air shimmered, the notes lingering longer than they should, vibrating with something more than resonance. The hair on her arms prickled... she wasn't alone. Around her images formed, as if emerging from a fog. She played on, faster now, keeping time with the beating of her heart.

Figures materialized, cloaked in hues of the ocean, shimmering like reflections. They were women, all standing proud, their hands resting on harps—harps identical to hers. They resembled her, their eyes deep as pools, faces bearing the serenity of someone who has always known the secrets of the tides.

The room filled with a sense of ancient waters, the scent of sea salt, the whisper of waves against distant shores. The figures played along with her, their music lacing through her own, creating harmonies she'd never imagined. They were her ancestors, Piscean muses who had called forth dreams, intuition, and emotion from the depths. She was *not* disconnected, *not* an accident. She was part of a lineage—one that swam deeply in the waters of creativity, empathy, and magic.

Her music transformed, and a warmth spread through her chest. The sense of belonging wrapped around her like an embrace. She was a daughter of water, a Pisces bound by generations to this magic, this music, this place.

She would never have to feel alone again.